Table of Contents
Word Problems
Grade 4

Being a Writer Is Such Fun! 2
Sports Activities Are Just Plain Great! 4
Now, That's a Lot of Groceries! 6
Let's Make Art Projects! 8
Carnivals and Fairs 10
Can You Save It Too? 12
Saving for What You Want Is Half the Fun! 14
There's a Time for Everything! 16
A Class Bowling Trip! 18
Do You Collect Things? 20
Let's Go Metal Detecting! 22
Science Is Exciting! 24
It's Time for the Show to Begin! 26
Yes We Can! Let's Raise the Money! 28
How Much? How Many? 30
What Fun We Have at School! 32
Reading Is Such a Fun Adventure! 34
Doesn't Money Add Up Fast? 36
Let's Go Out Where the Sun Shines! 38
Voting for the School Mascot! 40
It's Time to Munch! 42
Kids Can Make Money Too! 44
Let's Split These Up! 46
There's Always Something Going On at School! 48
Outdoors Can Be Fun Too! 50
Special Events for Kids! 52
Let's Have Fun at School! 54
Large Numbers Divide Up Just as Easily! 56
Fun Foods Are Just Plain "Fun!" 58
Division Takes Place Outside of Class Too! 60
What Is Your Favorite? 62
Field Trips Are Such a Blast! 64
And the Fraction Is 66
Have Fun With These! 68
Here's a Challenge for You! 70
Help-at-Home Activities 72

BEING A WRITER IS SUCH FUN!

1. 482 children from Charlie's school have pen pals in Europe! 391 children from Jeremy's school have pen pals in South America! How many children in all have fun writing to pen pals?

   873

2. There are 687 boys and girls at Rock Elementary School that love writing poetry! At Crooked Branch Junior High, 239 students have actually put their poems to music! How many students in all have written poetry?

   926

3. 527 boys and girls at David's school have sent in short stories to the school writing contest! 398 students have sent in autobiographies. How many students in all have entered the writing contest?

   925

4. At Peter's school, 279 students said they prefer to write with pens, and 446 said they prefer to write with pencils. How many students altogether like to write with pens and pencils?

   725

Addition of Whole Numbers

5. 368 boys and girls said that they write their grandparents as much as they can! 285 students said they write their cousins. Altogether, how many students write their grandparents and cousins?

6. Blue Mountain High School sold 3,942 pencils last year. So far this year, the school has sold 2,485. How many pencils have been sold in all?

7. For the contest to find a name for the zoo's new gorilla, 7,546 children sent in funny names and 3,229 children sent in serious names. How many children altogether sent in names for the gorilla?

8. There are 6,204 students in Tom's town that like to write stories about famous local heroes! But, there are 2,387 students that prefer to make up their own stories! How many students like to write in Tom's town?

9. 3,426 children signed up for the writing classes offered by the city! 2,635 signed up for the art classes being offered! How many children in all signed up for these classes?

SPORTS ACTIVITIES ARE JUST PLAIN GREAT!

1. 41 fourth graders, 35 fifth graders and 27 sixth graders showed up for practice. How many boys and girls attended altogether?

   103

2. 304 children from the east side, 294 from the south side and 238 from the north side showed up to register to play sports. How many children in all showed up to participate?

   836

3. 34 girls, 29 boys and 19 grown-ups came to ice skate on the frozen pond. How many people in all came to glide and dance on the ice?

   82

4. In the morning, there were 263 people using the ski lifts. By noon, there were another 352! By evening, another 174 had joined in to ski down the mountain. How many people in all came to ski?

   789

Addition of Whole Numbers

5. At the lake one bright, sunny day, there were 841 people swimming, 173 sailing and 329 playing on the sandy beach! How many people were at the lake having a great time?

   1,343

6. Pop Up Park had 4,238 boys show up to play baseball, Grounder Park had 6,052, and Home Run Park had 1,879. How many boys altogether showed up to play?

   12,169

7. This year, 4,740 girls came regularly to gymnastics. Last year, 5,286 girls came. The year before, 2,958 girls came. How many girls in all have enjoyed gymnastics in the last three years?

   12,984

8. Mia's city swimming league had 7,369 boys and girls that swam on its teams. Joan's city league had 3,564 boys and girls that swam. Lacy's city league had 6,350. How many boys and girls swam on swim teams in these three leagues?

   7,283

9. Of all the fourth graders at camp, 47 wanted to learn archery, 68 wanted to learn orienteering, and 72 wanted to go horseback riding! How many students in all wanted to learn different activities?

   187

NOW, THAT'S A LOT OF GROCERIES!

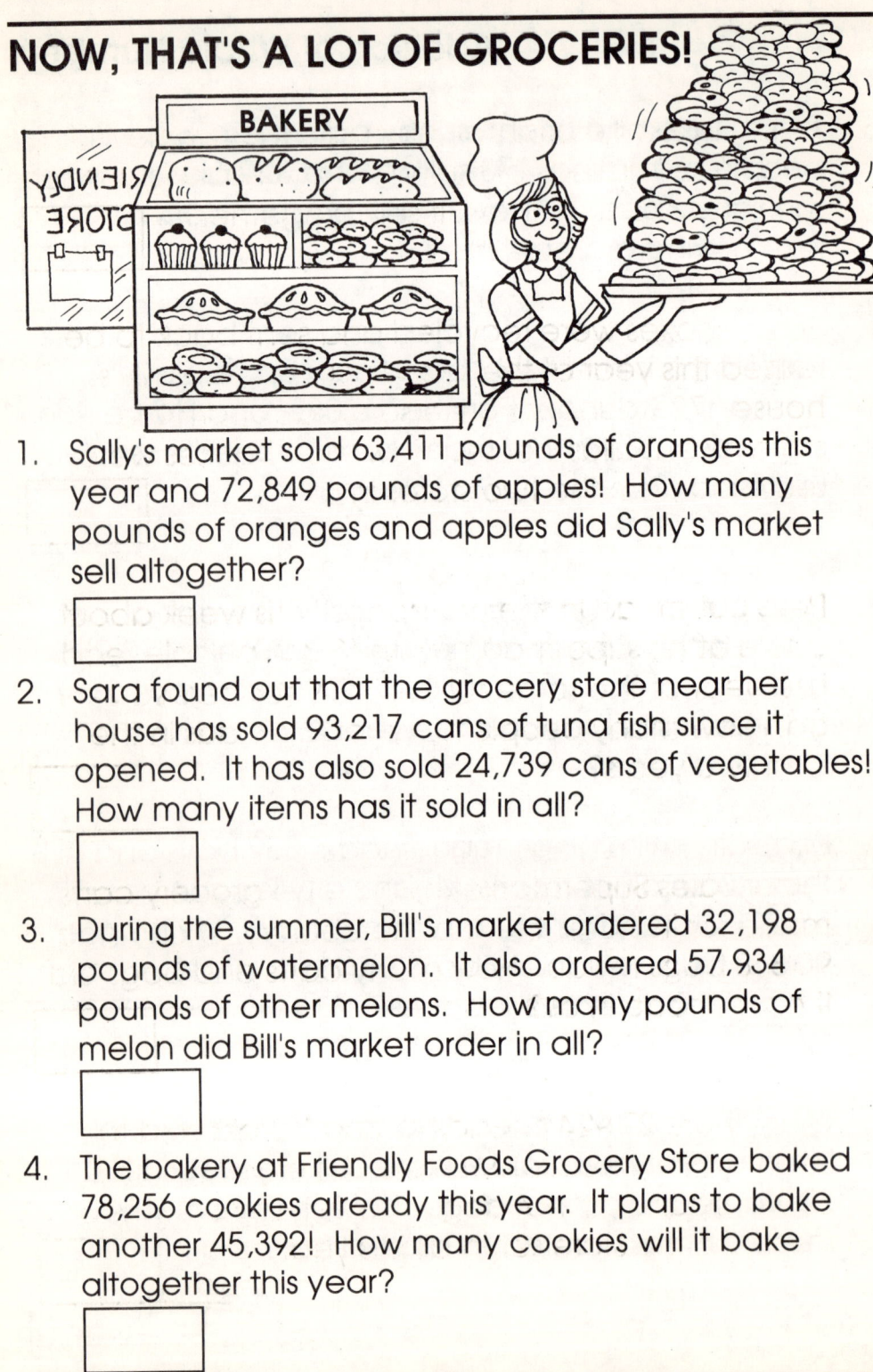

1. Sally's market sold 63,411 pounds of oranges this year and 72,849 pounds of apples! How many pounds of oranges and apples did Sally's market sell altogether?

2. Sara found out that the grocery store near her house has sold 93,217 cans of tuna fish since it opened. It has also sold 24,739 cans of vegetables! How many items has it sold in all?

3. During the summer, Bill's market ordered 32,198 pounds of watermelon. It also ordered 57,934 pounds of other melons. How many pounds of melon did Bill's market order in all?

4. The bakery at Friendly Foods Grocery Store baked 78,256 cookies already this year. It plans to bake another 45,392! How many cookies will it bake altogether this year?

Addition of Whole Numbers

5. Fresh Foods, Inc. sold 34,786 gallons of whole milk and 46,270 gallons of skim milk this year. How much whole and skim milk did it sell altogether?

6. 98,251 boxes were recycled and sent back to be reused this year at the supermarket near Sally's house. 72,838 boxes were sent back from the store near Dallas' house. How many boxes were recycled from the two stores in all?

7. Pete put an ad in the newspaper this week about a sale at his supermarket that 68,345 people read. Last year at the same time, 58,279 readers saw his ad. How many people have read his ads in the past two years?

8. Super Sales Supermarket had 67,246 grocery carts made for its stores around the country. It also had 90,868 bags made. How many carts and bags did it have made in all?

9. There were 27,924 pounds of hamburger sold this year by Bill's Discount Market. The store also sold 56,387 pounds of hot dogs. How many pounds of meat did the store sell in all this year?

LET'S MAKE ART PROJECTS!

1. 83 students at Debbie's school wanted to learn about making pottery! 57 asked to learn about leatherwork. How many more students asked to learn about making pottery?

   [26]

2. 50 students said they would like to weave on the looms in the classroom. 34 students said they would prefer to work with papier-mâché. How many more wanted to work on the looms?

   [84]

3. Miss June's students made 507 baskets. They also made 345 pieces of pottery. How many more baskets did they make?

   [182]

4. Mr. Mark's students used 292 sheets of colored construction paper to make their creative cards. They also used 148 pieces of chalk. How much more paper did they use?

   [144]

Word Problems IF0193 ©1992 Instructional Fair, Inc.

Subtraction of Whole Numbers

5. At the art show, Sam's Creek Elementary School displayed 723 sculptures and 435 paintings. How many more sculptures did it display?

6. Eva's school had a total of 456 students who brought in used magazines to help make the collages during art class. 278 students brought in old newspapers. How many more students brought in magazines?

7. Mr. Swanson was really impressed that 67 students in the fourth grade preferred to paint pictures of the school with water colors. 49 students wanted to paint with tempera paints. How many more students wanted to use water colors?

8. 72 students came after school to help make the life-size papier-mâché dinosaur! 35 students came to work on the scenery for the school play. How many more came to work on the dinosaur?

9. Teresa's school ordered 258 paintbrushes for the school year. The school also ordered 162 drawing pencils. How many more paintbrushes did it order?

CARNIVALS AND FAIRS

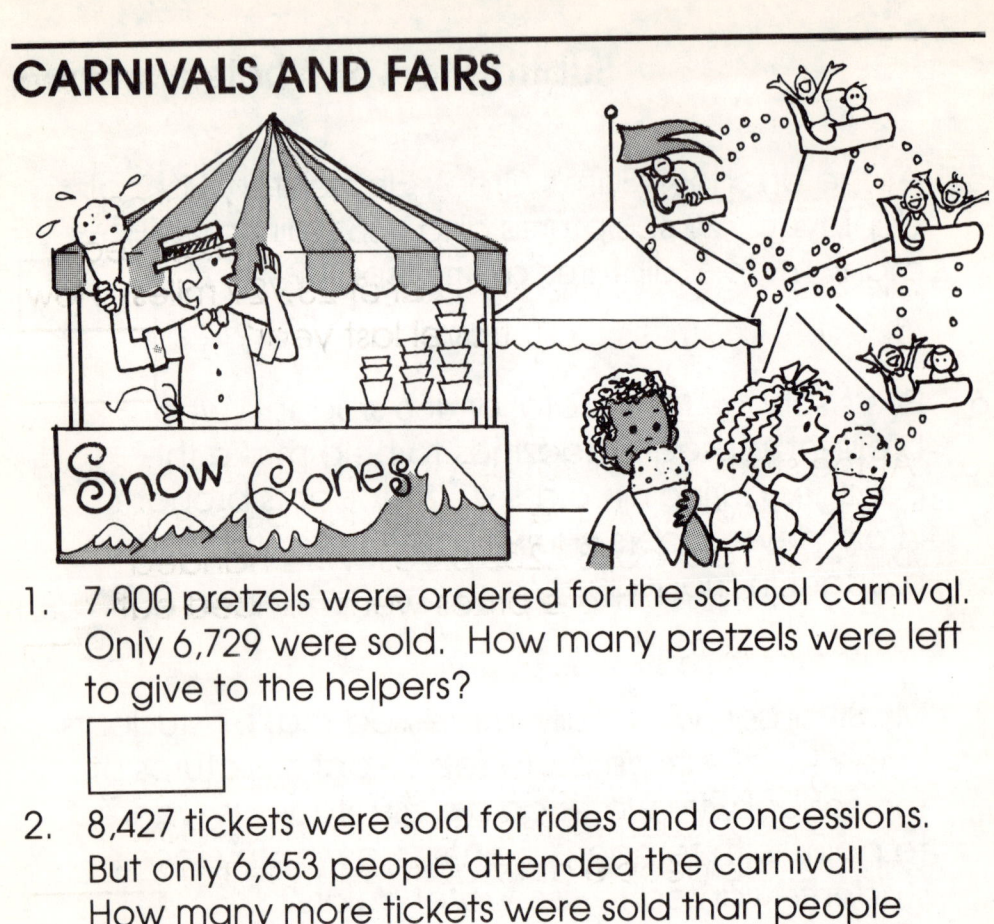

1. 7,000 pretzels were ordered for the school carnival. Only 6,729 were sold. How many pretzels were left to give to the helpers?

2. 8,427 tickets were sold for rides and concessions. But only 6,653 people attended the carnival! How many more tickets were sold than people attended?

3. The Ferris wheel weighed 79,467 pounds. The bumper car ride weighed 58,628 pounds. How much more did the Ferris wheel weigh?

4. Helpers working at the concession stand used 1,472 pounds of ice to make snow cones. They also used 976 cups to serve them. How much more ice was used than cups?

Subtraction of Whole Numbers

5. The visiting carnival company at our school has already traveled 15,324 miles this year. Last year, the company traveled a total of 23,729 miles. How many more miles did it travel last year?

6. At the state fair, 56,324 prizes were given to people who attended. At the carnival, just before the company arrived, 39,252 prizes were handed out. How many more prizes were handed out at the state fair?

7. 98,245 people attended the state fair this year. 78,372 people attended the county fair. How many more people attended the state fair?

8. 7,239 balloons were handed out in one day at the state fair. On the same day, 5,287 hot dogs were served. How many more balloons were handed out?

9. At the state fair this year, there were 6,234 animal, art, plant and music exhibits to see. At the same fair last year, there was a total of 5,382 exhibits. How many more exhibits were at the state fair this year?

CAN YOU SAVE IT TOO?

1. Alex and his dad went to the store to buy fishing equipment for their trip. They bought a fishing pole for $7.95, weights and hooks for $.98 and a net for $2.31. How much did they spend in all?

2. Deborah spent $24.97 for a new dress and $9.24 for a flower corsage to wear to her piano recital. How much did she spend to look nice for the recital?

3. Andy was really excited about learning to speak French. He went to the bookstore and bought a book on French that cost $9.46, a tape set that cost $12.59 and a set of flash cards that cost $6.39. How much money did he spend in all?

4. Dwight wanted to learn to skateboard. So he went down to the store and bought a skateboard for $86.78, a helmet for $35.37 and kneepads for $23.00. How much did he spend in all to enjoy this sport?

Addition of Money

5. Joan and Lois wanted to make their report about their state look really sharp! So they bought poster board for $.98, markers for $2.59 and postcards with great pictures of their state for $.63. How much did they spend in all?

6. Barbara found out that to fly to visit her cousins would cost $45.27. Also, the bus from the airport to their city would be an additional $27.35. How much would it cost Barbara in all to visit her cousins?

7. Richard spent $.36 on felt, $.79 on bug eyes and $.86 on glue for his craft project. How much did he spend altogether?

8. Lucy, Jennifer and Elizabeth decided to buy lunch while they were shopping at the mall. The pizza cost $4.80, the milks came to $2.67, and the fresh fruit cost $1.34. How much did they spend on lunch at the mall?

9. James needed a few kits for the scout meeting. He bought a crystal radio kit for $10.89, a model rocket kit for $7.45 and a compass and canteen kit for $5.38. How much did he spend in all for the kits?

SAVING FOR WHAT YOU WANT IS HALF THE FUN!

1. When Rob and his family went out for pizza, it cost them $18.43. When they went out for hamburgers, it cost them $15.56. How much more did it cost to go out for pizza?

2. Maria had $84.23 to spend on a new cassette player. She found just the one she wanted for $76.46. How much did she receive in change?

3. Walter and his brother Dan wanted to see the rings of Saturn with their very own telescope. Together, they had a total of $85.04. The telescope they picked out sold for $54.23. How much money did they have left to save?

4. Sue's pen pal letter to England cost her $.67 in postage. Nancy's letter cost her $.48. How much more did Sue spend on postage for her letter?

Subtraction of Money

5. Calvin's new baseball glove cost him $24.78. His new bat only cost $8.59. How much more did he spend for the glove?

6. Spencer and his sister Jennifer went miniature golfing. This cost a total of $8.60. After they were done, they played a few games of air hockey that cost them another $1.75. How much more did they spend playing miniature golf?

7. Margaret's parents paid a total of $87.46 to buy her a new guitar. They also spent $9.27 to sign her up for group lessons at the community center. How much more did they spend for the guitar?

8. To rent a violin for one year cost David's family $95.62. Eva's parents paid $86.43 to rent a flute for one year. How much more did it cost David's family to rent the violin?

9. To rent a hotel on the beach, Samuel's parents paid a total of $97.50. It only cost them $43.24 to rent a car. How much more did they spend for the hotel on the beach?

THERE'S A TIME FOR EVERYTHING!

Leah rises in the morning.　　Gwen leaves for school.　　Carlos goes to bed.

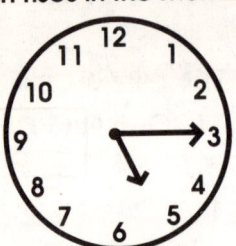  

Mark starts to　　　　　　　David starts　　　　　　　Eva starts her
practice the piano.　　　　to eat lunch.　　　　　　　homework.

  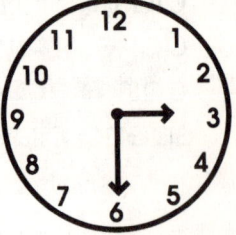

1. How long is it from the time Mark starts practicing piano until Gwen leaves for school?

   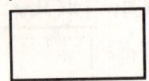

2. David's lunch and recess are over at 12:00 p.m. How long does he have for lunch?

   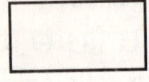

3. Eva eats dinner $2\frac{1}{2}$ hours after she starts her homework. What time does her family sit down for dinner?

   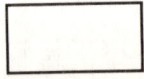

4. David's school ends at 3:00 p.m. How long is it from the time he starts lunch until he goes home at the end of the day?

   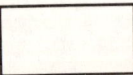

Time

5. Leah likes to exercise for one hour after she rises in the morning! What time does she finish exercising?

6. Mark's school starts at 9:00 a.m. His first class starts 15 minutes after school begins. How long is it from when he starts piano practice until the time his first class starts?

7. Gwen gets up in the morning at 7:00 a.m. How long is it before she leaves for school?

8. Carlos loves to read books from 7:25 p.m. until it's time for him to go to bed! How long does he like to read books?

9. David's reading class starts at 10:20 a.m. If this class ends 5 minutes before lunch time, how long does his reading class last?

A CLASS BOWLING TRIP!

1. When the students got to the bowling alley, 4 of them used special 6-pound balls. How many pounds did this equal altogether?

2. Three students each knocked down 4 pins on their first balls. How many pins did they knock down in all?

3. Four students asked to have bumpers put in their lanes to keep the balls from rolling in the gutters. If each lane had to have 2 bumpers, how many bumpers had to be blown up in all?

4. These boys and girls were really good bowlers. Eight of them each had 5 spares. How many spares did this total in all?

Multiplication of Whole Numbers

5. Not only did some students have spares, but 9 students each had 2 strikes! Now that's downright awesome!! How many strikes did these 9 students have altogether?

6. Five students each decided to play 3 games. How many games did they have to pay for altogether?

7. Seven students were each able to keep the ball going right down the center of the lane 4 times in a row! How many times were they able to keep the ball straight in all?

8. At the start of the next game, 2 students were each able to knock down 8 pins on their first tries! How many pins did they knock down altogether?

9. In the last frame, 5 students each knocked down 5 pins on their second balls! How many pins did they knock down altogether with their second balls?

DO YOU COLLECT THINGS?

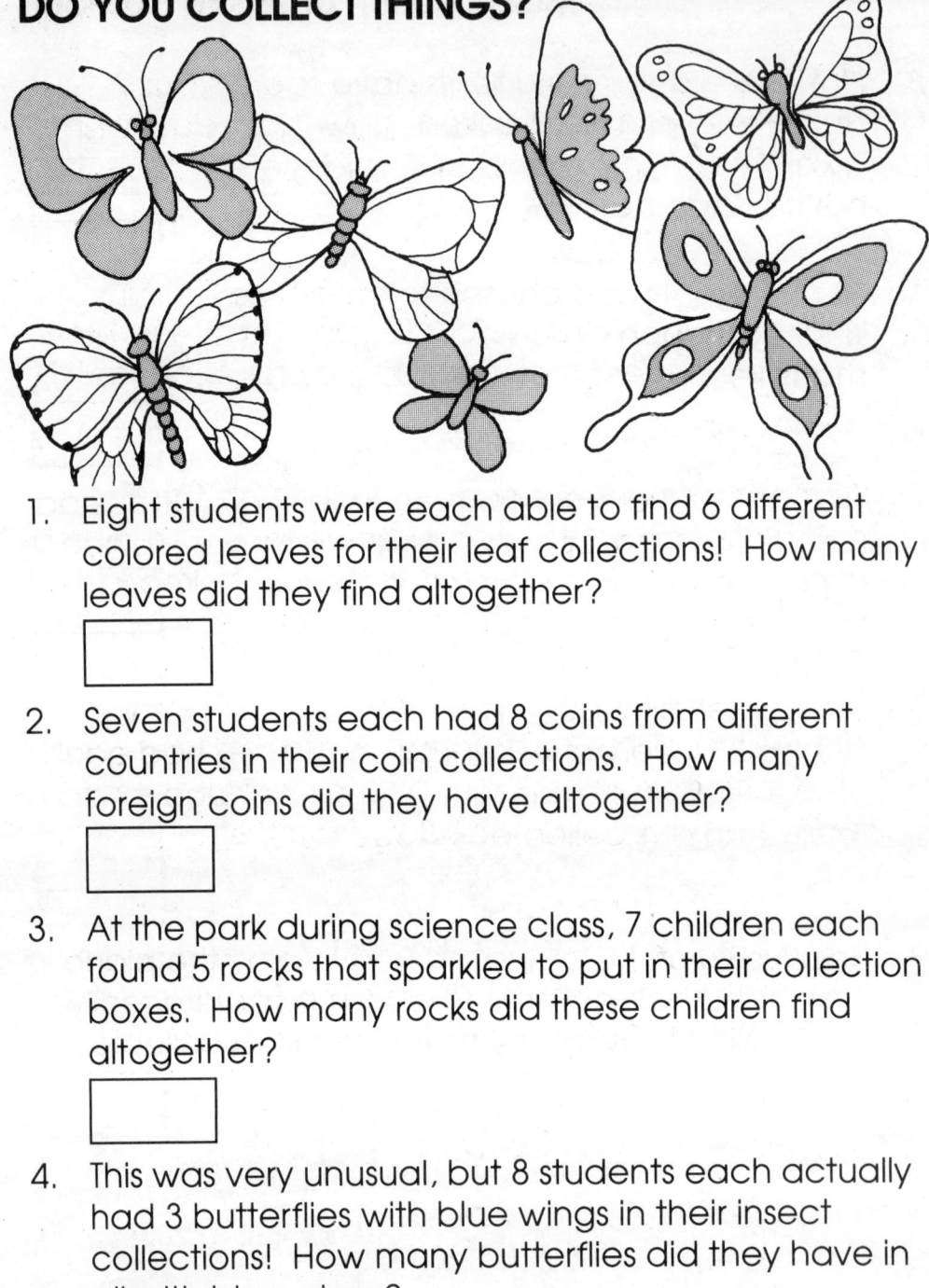

1. Eight students were each able to find 6 different colored leaves for their leaf collections! How many leaves did they find altogether?

2. Seven students each had 8 coins from different countries in their coin collections. How many foreign coins did they have altogether?

3. At the park during science class, 7 children each found 5 rocks that sparkled to put in their collection boxes. How many rocks did these children find altogether?

4. This was very unusual, but 8 students each actually had 3 butterflies with blue wings in their insect collections! How many butterflies did they have in all with blue wings?

Multiplication of Whole Numbers

5. Eleven students each had 6 rookie cards in their baseball card collections! How many rookie cards did they have altogether?

6. Nine students had chosen to collect key chains. They had each collected 7 key chains so far. How many key chains had they collected altogether?

7. Six children were collecting neat pencils. They had each collected 5 pencils. How many pencils had they collected to this point altogether?

8. Five students loved to read so much that they decided to collect exciting books. They had each collected 9 mystery books. How many books had these students collected altogether?

9. Because 6 of the children loved to play the piano, they had each collected 6 songs that were really fun to play! How many songs had they collected altogether?

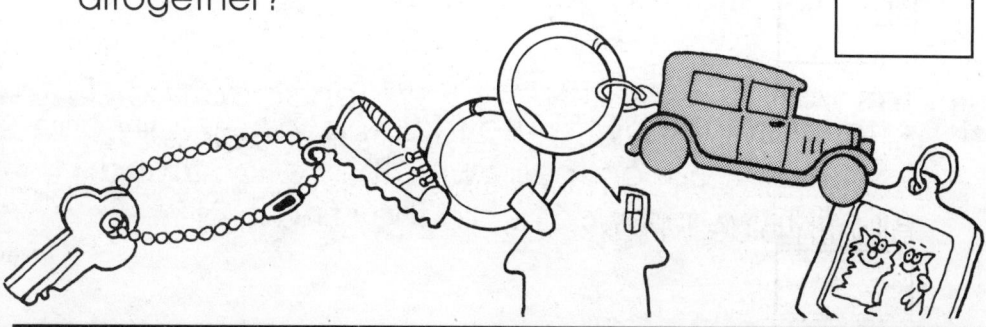

Word Problems IF0193

LET'S GO METAL DETECTING!

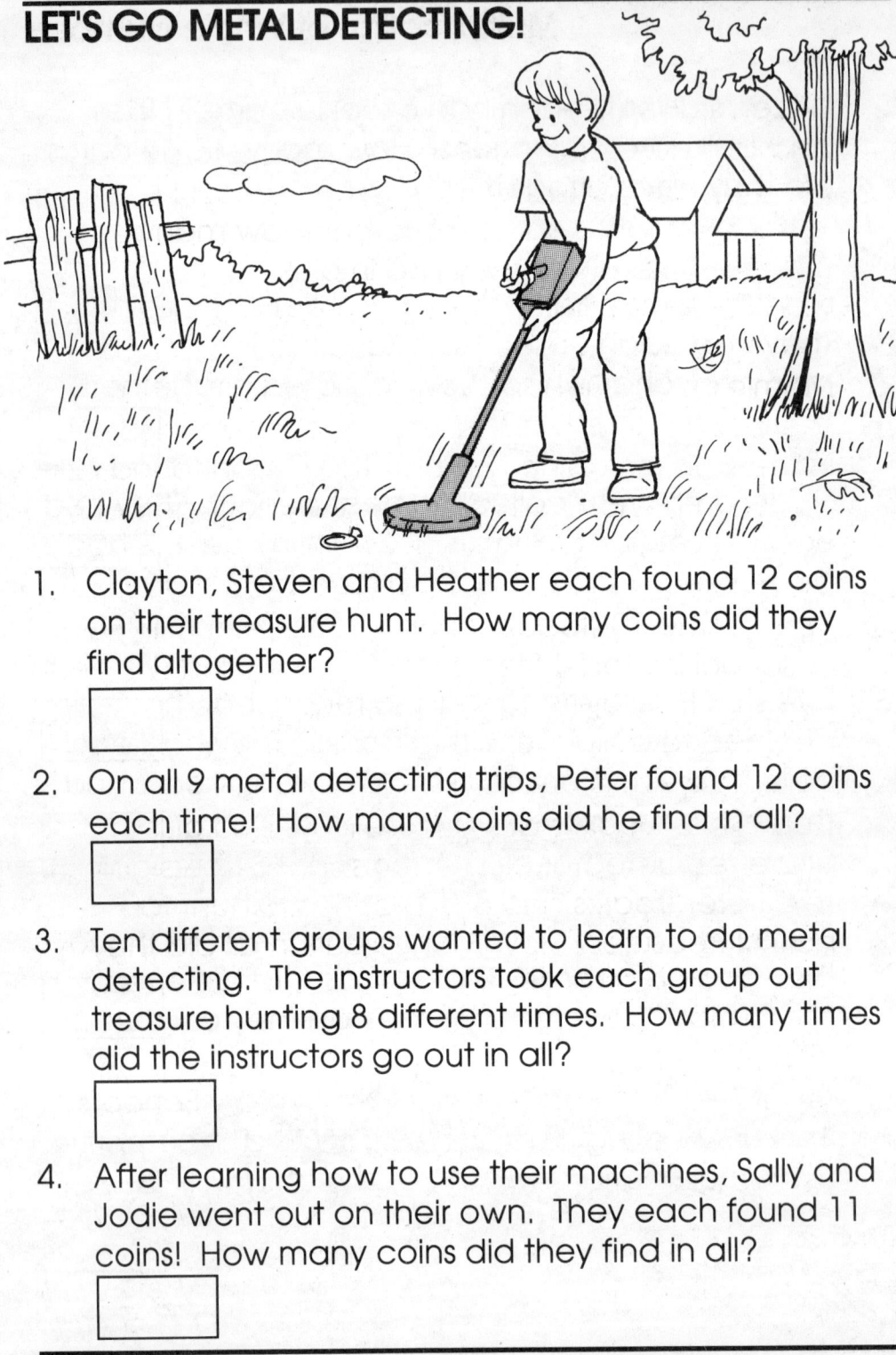

1. Clayton, Steven and Heather each found 12 coins on their treasure hunt. How many coins did they find altogether?

2. On all 9 metal detecting trips, Peter found 12 coins each time! How many coins did he find in all?

3. Ten different groups wanted to learn to do metal detecting. The instructors took each group out treasure hunting 8 different times. How many times did the instructors go out in all?

4. After learning how to use their machines, Sally and Jodie went out on their own. They each found 11 coins! How many coins did they find in all?

Multiplication of Whole Numbers

5. All 11 boys in Earl's scout troop wanted to go out and hunt for treasure. They each found 11 interesting things on their search! How many pieces of metal did they find in all?

6. Mamie's treasure hunting club went to the park to see what it could find. There were 8 boys and girls in the club including her, and they each found 12 coins. How many coins did they find altogether?

7. Each of the 10 students in the treasure hunting club at school invited 4 friends to join. How many friends in all did they invite to join their club?

8. During the weekend, 11 of the boys and girls in Marlene's detector club each spent 6 hours going to different parks and playgrounds to hunt for buried treasures. How many hours in all did they go out during the weekend?

9. Ten students in Beaver Creek Elementary School's treasure hunting club had each found 3 meteorites using their metal detectors. How many meteorites had they found altogether?

SCIENCE IS EXCITING!

1. Eight classrooms got to make solar ovens. There were 32 students in each classroom. How many students in all had fun using the heat from the sun to cook food?

2. Three schools started recycling clubs to help the environment. Each club had 67 boys and girls as members. How many students joined altogether?

3. Mr. Melamed's 6 science classes each learned how to find the dew point. There were 29 boys and girls in each group. How many students in all learned how to find the dew point?

4. 97 students each brought in 2 lemons to make batteries on Monday. How many lemons did they bring in altogether?

Multiplication of Whole Numbers

5. Five groups went on the overnight to do science outdoors in the mountains. There were 73 students in each group. What was the total number of students that went on the overnight?

6. For the crystal growing project, 4 students each brought in 18 glass jars for the other students to share. How many glass jars did they bring in altogether?

7. In the district where Nicole goes to school, 7 schools signed up to have model rocket clubs. 48 boys and girls from each school wanted to be part of the fun! How many students in all will be building and launching rockets?

8. Eight students who entered the science fair had seashell collections! Each collection contained 64 seashells of all different types. How many shells were there altogether?

9. Two students each brought in 49 straws to share with the class so that they could demonstrate how a vacuum works. How many straws did they bring in altogether?

IT'S TIME FOR THE SHOW TO BEGIN!

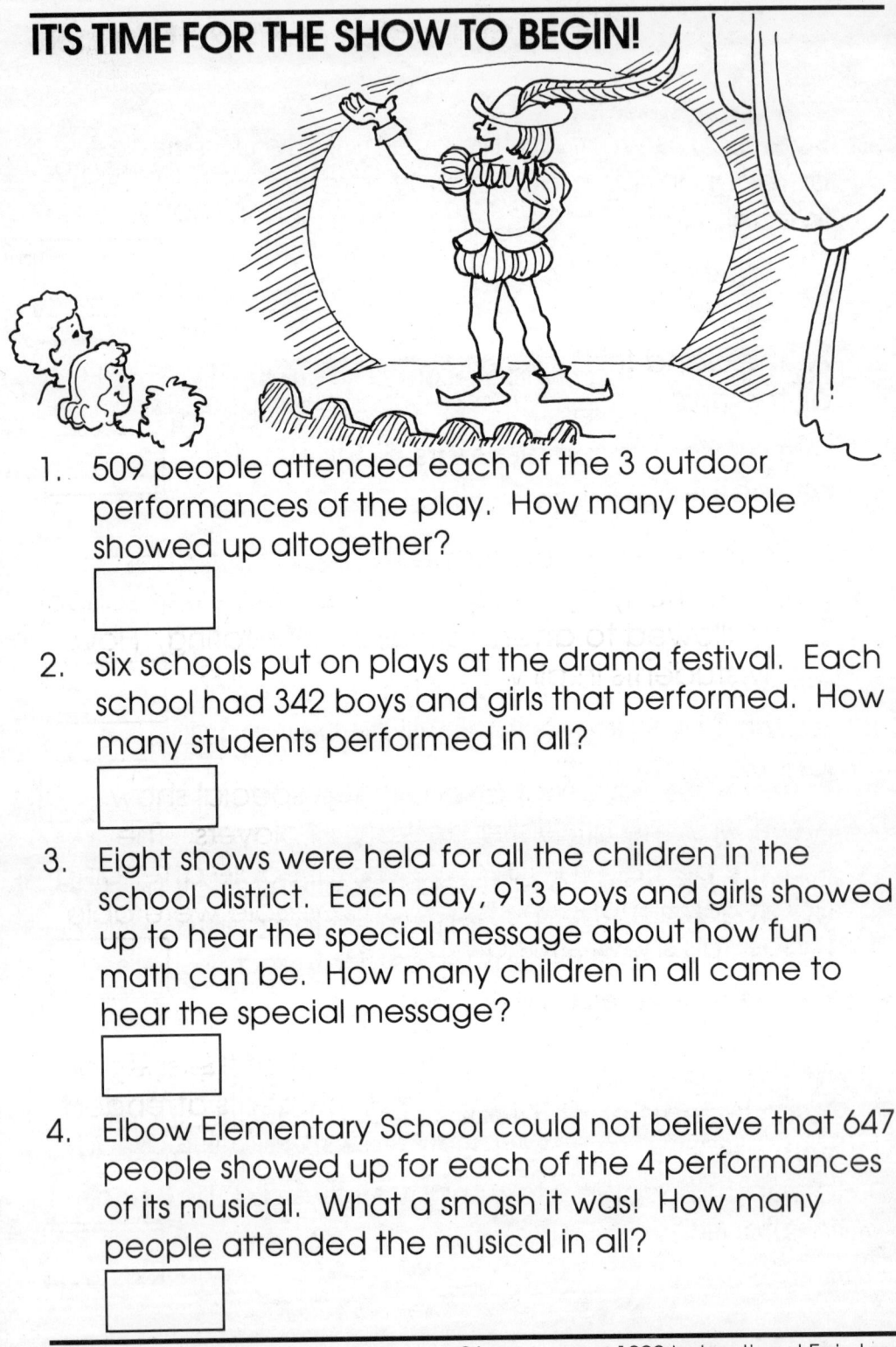

1. 509 people attended each of the 3 outdoor performances of the play. How many people showed up altogether?

2. Six schools put on plays at the drama festival. Each school had 342 boys and girls that performed. How many students performed in all?

3. Eight shows were held for all the children in the school district. Each day, 913 boys and girls showed up to hear the special message about how fun math can be. How many children in all came to hear the special message?

4. Elbow Elementary School could not believe that 647 people showed up for each of the 4 performances of its musical. What a smash it was! How many people attended the musical in all?

Multiplication of Whole Numbers

5. All 218 members of the musical cast each invited 9 people to attend their new show. How many people did they invite in all?

6. At the band festival, 6 different states showed up for all the fun. Each state entered 748 musicians. How many musicians got to play in this festival?

7. Five different schools came to hear the orchestra from Germany. Only 263 students from each school were allowed to attend because of seating. How many students in all were able to attend?

8. There were 7 performances of the special show hosted by the city's star basketball players. The activity center was filled with 537 people attending each performance. How many people were able to see this show altogether?

9. Sharla's school held 2 performances of the special puppet show on fire safety. 429 students attended each assembly. How many students in all learned about fire safety?

YES WE CAN! LET'S RAISE THE MONEY!

1. David and Bill each found 3,028 aluminum cans to sell. How many cans did they find in all?

   6,056

2. All 6 schools that entered the fund-raising drive each sold 4,721 school banners. How many banners were sold in all?

   28,326

3. Three students each rocked back and forth 5,918 times in the schoolwide "rockathon!" How many times did they rock back and forth in the rocking chairs altogether?

   17,754

4. Nine boys and girls each signed up 2,764 people who said they would donate a penny a mile for their "climb up the mountain" fund raiser. How many people did they sign up altogether?

   18

Multiplication of Whole Numbers

5. Four cities each signed up 8,913 helpers to gather and collect items for the huge rummage sale. How many helpers signed up in all? 35,[?]

6. Each of the 7 families turned in 2,746 pounds of newspaper to help pay for the new computer software! How many pounds of newspaper did they turn in altogether? 1[?]

7. Five classes each sold 3,842 name tags to help pay for the new playground equipment. How many name tags did they sell in all? 1,[?]210

8. Two schools in Bobby's city each donated 9,784 pounds of food for those in need. How many pounds of food did they donate altogether? 19,568

9. 6,972 people showed up for each of the 8 performances of the special rodeo to help fund the new gymnasium. How many people in all attended the rodeo? 75,[?]

HOW MUCH? HOW MANY?

1. Kent sent 8 letters that each weighed 0.75 ounces. How much did his letters weigh altogether?

   6.00

2. James bought 3 large jars of peanut butter for the trip to camp. Each jar weighed 2.49 kilograms. How many kilograms did they weigh altogether?

   7.47

3. Tammy's saddle weighed a total of 87.46 pounds. How much would 6 of these saddles weigh?

   524.76

4. It takes Kathryn 14.39 minutes to ride her bike to school each day. How many minutes does she spend in 5 days traveling to school on her bike?

   71.95

Multiplication of Decimals

5. Timothy filled 2 water tanks that each held 8.79 gallons for the long camping trip. How many gallons did he fill in all?

6. Four children each brought backpacks on the hike that weighed 27.09 kilograms. How many kilograms did their backpacks weigh in all?

   108.36

7. While at the movies, 9 students each bought a package of peanuts that weighed 0.76 pounds. How much did their peanuts weigh altogether?

   6.84

8. Edward ordered 5 basketballs by mail. Each one weighed 2.43 pounds. What was the total weight of the basketballs?

   12.15

9. Bruce flies 34.19 kilometers 8 times each month in his helicopter. How many total kilometers does he fly each month?

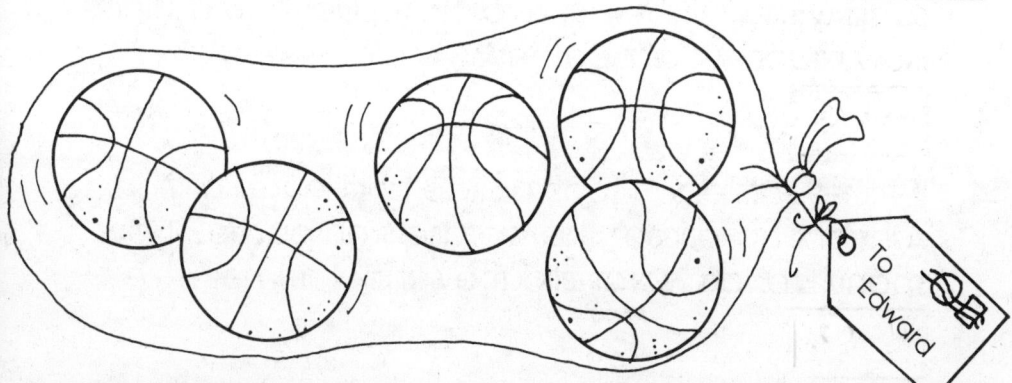

Word Problems IF0193 ©1992 Instructional Fair, Inc.

WHAT FUN WE HAVE AT SCHOOL!

1. 23 students each brought in 89 jokes and riddles that they had made up. How many did they bring in altogether?

2. All 35 students in Mr. Brown's math class each did the 56-problem obstacle course. How many problems did they do in all?

3. 82 children each signed up to memorize the funny song with 47 lines in music class. How many lines did they learn altogether?

4. 69 students each took on the challenge of finding 41 French words in the wordsearch puzzle. How many French words did they look for in all?

Multiplication of Whole Numbers

5. Each of the 58 children that looked for the 67 things wrong with the funny picture found every one of them. It was a challenge, but a blast too! How many things wrong with the crazy picture did they find altogether?

6. 91 boys and girls zoomed through the 26 hours that they were each required to spend reading last month. That's never a problem when you just love to read! How many hours in all did they read books?

7. 74 children each entered the exciting math championship that involved a test with 63 very challenging problems on it. Everyone was proven a champion that day! How many problems did they complete in all?

8. All 33 students had the privilege of reading Pablo's book of cartoons and funny stories. If each student read all 18 pages, how many pages did they read altogether?

9. All 38 students in Mrs. Wiley's art class were required to draw 21 different crazy characters to use in their cartoon strips. How many funny people did they create in all?

READING IS SUCH A FUN ADVENTURE!

1. Each of the 27 students in Mr. Schmidt's class read the 384-page book about tongue twisters. How many pages did they read altogether?

2. So far at Greenfield Elementary School, 41 boys and girls have read the joke book with 823 funny and hilarious jokes to make you laugh. If all 41 students have read every joke, how many jokes have they read in all?

3. 521 of the students at Jerry's school have each read the 73 cartoon books in the library. How many times in all have the books been checked out?

4. 928 students over the past five years have each checked out all 90 of the science books on astronomy. How many times in all have the books been checked out?

Multiplication of Whole Numbers

5. 35 schools in Brussels Sprout County each have 736 books set aside just for fourth graders. How many books does the county have set aside in all for fourth graders?

6. 64 boys and girls from fourth grade have each read 182 exciting and fun books this year. How many books have they enjoyed reading in all?

7. There are 485 students at Fluffy Cloud Elementary School that have each read 24 of the funny animal books in the library. Everyone's favorite is the interesting book on cute little muskrats. How many times have these books been read altogether?

8. Sixteen students had each read a total of 508 pages by October. Their teacher was so happy to see them reading and having fun! How many pages had they read in all by October?

9. 57 of the children that each read the 238-page book on incredible records around the world loved every page they read. What is the total number of pages that they loved reading?

DOESN'T MONEY ADD UP FAST?

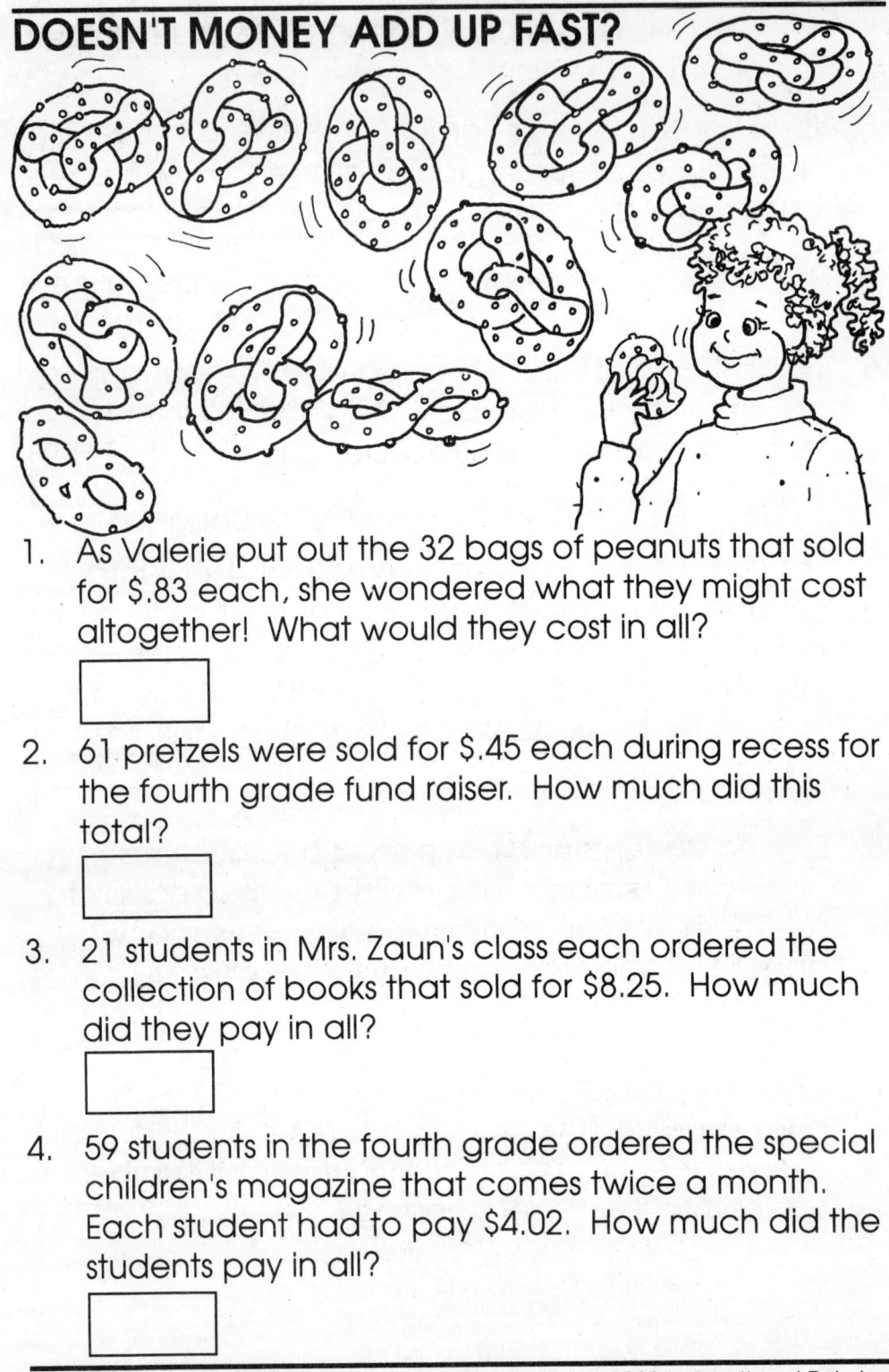

1. As Valerie put out the 32 bags of peanuts that sold for $.83 each, she wondered what they might cost altogether! What would they cost in all?

2. 61 pretzels were sold for $.45 each during recess for the fourth grade fund raiser. How much did this total?

3. 21 students in Mrs. Zaun's class each ordered the collection of books that sold for $8.25. How much did they pay in all?

4. 59 students in the fourth grade ordered the special children's magazine that comes twice a month. Each student had to pay $4.02. How much did the students pay in all?

Multiplication of Money

5. The student council sold a total of 49 school binders for $2.13 each. How much money did the student council raise altogether?

6. Monica counted 19 people buying the special new pencils that write both in pen and pencil at the flick of a switch! Each one sold for $3.12. How much did these people pay in all for these pencils?

7. 26 people on the bus to camp each bought a pack of sugarless gum for $.61. How much did they pay in all for their gum?

8. All 58 people that went on the field trip to the train museum had to pay an admission price of $2.95. How much did they pay altogether?

9. Dale's mom bought 84 juicy, crisp, red apples as a treat for his class on his birthday! The apples sold for $.26 each. How much did she pay in all?

LET'S GO OUT WHERE THE SUN SHINES!

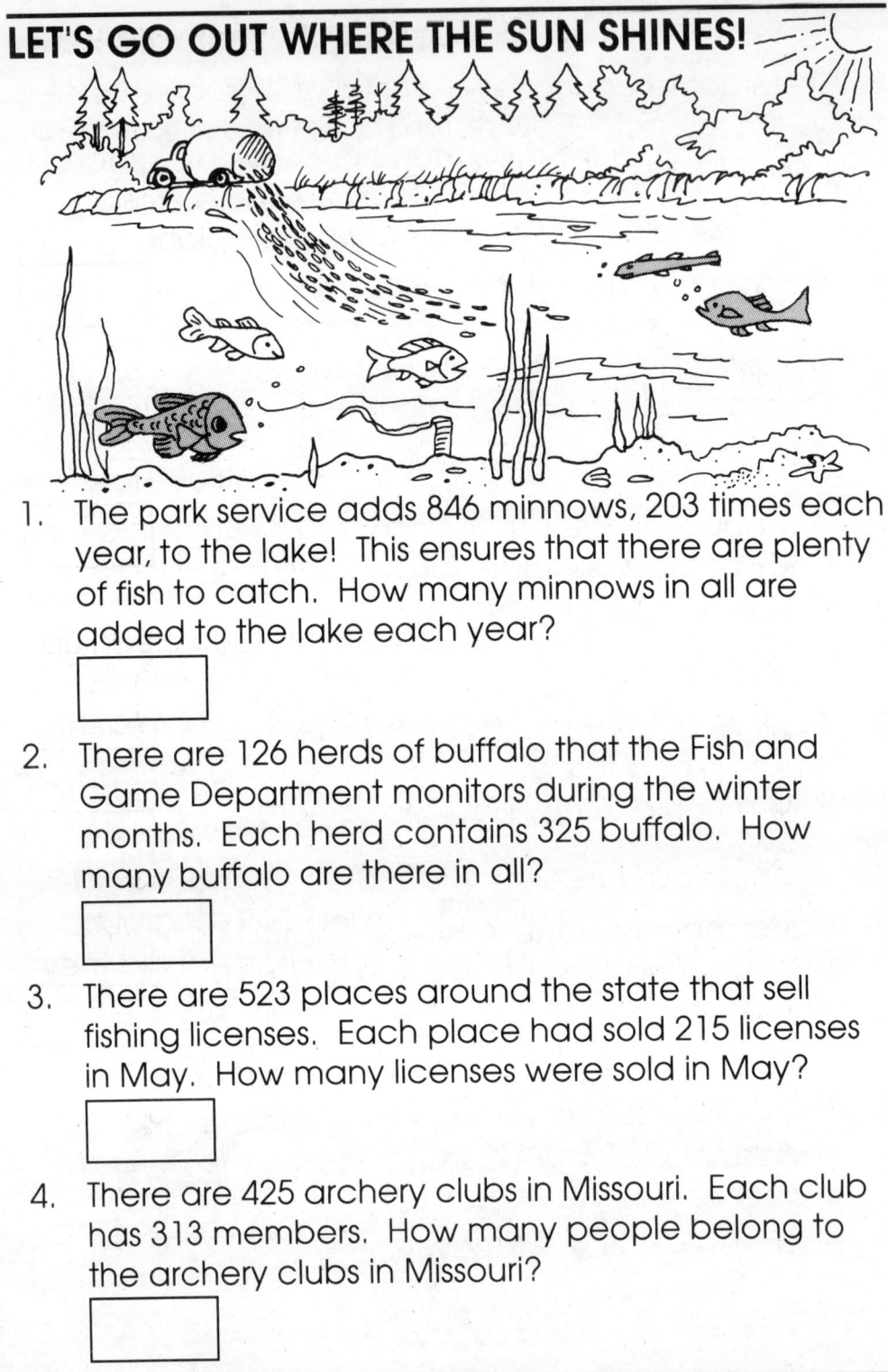

1. The park service adds 846 minnows, 203 times each year, to the lake! This ensures that there are plenty of fish to catch. How many minnows in all are added to the lake each year?

2. There are 126 herds of buffalo that the Fish and Game Department monitors during the winter months. Each herd contains 325 buffalo. How many buffalo are there in all?

3. There are 523 places around the state that sell fishing licenses. Each place had sold 215 licenses in May. How many licenses were sold in May?

4. There are 425 archery clubs in Missouri. Each club has 313 members. How many people belong to the archery clubs in Missouri?

Multiplication of Whole Numbers

5. To prevent soil erosion, the forest service planted 412 trees in each of the 247 spots where erosion had occurred. How many trees did it plant in all?

6. A total of 117 schools has each donated 452 helpers to go out and make sure all the lakes around the state are clean and beautiful. How many helpers are there in all?

7. 318 groups went out on Saturday to help clean up the parks and highways. Each group picked up 147 bags of litter. How many bags of trash did the groups pick up in all?

8. 305 baseball clubs each donated 224 pounds of grass seed for the different baseball fields around the city. How many pounds of grass seed did they donate altogether?

9. There are 654 families that each donated 183 pounds of aluminum cans to help pay for the new soccer field in the park. How many pounds did they contribute altogether?

VOTING FOR THE SCHOOL MASCOT!

Number of Votes for Each Animal

Animal	Votes
Bull	🐻🐻🐻🐻🐻🐻
Lion	🐻🐻🐻🐻🐻🐻🐻🐻🐻🐻
Mustang	🐻🐻
Cougar	🐻🐻🐻🐻🐻🐻🐻
Wildcat	🐻🐻 🐻🐻
Colt	🐻🐻🐻🐻🐻🐻🐻🐻🐻🐻🐻
Eagle	🐻🐻🐻🐻🐻🐻🐻🐻🐻
Cardinal	🐻
Panther	🐻🐻🐻 🐻🐻

Each 🐻 stands for 4 votes!

1. What is the total number of votes that the cougar, bull and wildcat received?

2. Which animal received the most votes?

3. How many more votes did the colt receive than the cougar?

4. What is the difference between the number of votes the most popular animal received and the least popular animal received?

Word Problems IF0193

Using a Pictograph

5. How many people cast their votes in all?

6. Which amount is more, the sum of the colt and eagle votes, or the sum of the bull, cougar and cardinal votes?

7. If 5 times as many people had voted for the lion, how many votes would it have received?

8. How many more people voted for the colt than for the wildcat?

9. Which animal would you vote for to be the school mascot? Why?

IT'S TIME TO MUNCH!

1. Bill's mom had a dish of 24 apple slices waiting when he and his friends returned from the baseball game! If there were 4 boys in all, how many slices did each boy receive?

   | 6 |

2. Theresa's mom brought in 36 pieces of fresh cantaloupe for the 9 girls at the slumber party. How many pieces did each girl receive?

   | 4 |

3. Carl's dad brought 48 granola bars along on the overnight backpacking trip for the 12 boys to have as energy snacks. How many bars did each boy receive?

   | 4 |

4. A total of 60 fresh strawberries was served at Jerry's swimming party. Each child received 5 strawberries to enjoy. How many children were at the party?

   | 12 |

Division of Whole Numbers

5. During the scout meeting, Doug's mom brought out a tray of 81 "bumps on a log" for the boys to enjoy. If there were 9 boys, how many did each boy get to munch on?

   9

6. During the movie party, Ralph's dad served his friends a tray full of 42 miniature pizzas. Since there were 7 children in all at the party, how many tiny pizzas did each child receive?

   6

7. All 12 members of the soccer team showed up for the end of the season picnic. The cooler had 24 drinks for the children to enjoy. How many drinks did each child have?

   2

8. Eight children were invited to Cyndi's birthday party. She made 48 cookies to share with her friends. How many cookies did each of her friends receive?

9. Carolyn made a total of 30 crackers topped with cheese and pepperoni bits for her friends to munch on during the talent show rehearsal. If each friend received 5 crackers, how many friends were at the rehearsal?

   6

KIDS CAN MAKE MONEY TOO!

1. Alecia and her brother and sister earned a total of $22 selling old toys at their family carport sale. How many dollars did each child receive? How much extra money did they have to divide up?

2. Joey and Sandy picked 17 baskets of blackberries to sell! What equal number of baskets did they pick? How many extra baskets did Sandy pick?

3. Diana sold a total of 35 silk flowers over 8 days. How many flowers did she sell each day? How many extras did she sell on one of the days?

4. Avery found 21 generous people to pledge money for his mountain "climbathon" to help the local food bank. He spent 4 days finding people to pledge. How many people did he find each day? How many extras did he find on one of the days?

Division of Whole Numbers

5. Robin and Sean collected 27 pounds of aluminum cans 5 different times. How many pounds did they find each time? How many extra pounds did they find one time?

6. Marty's class sold a total of 38 craft projects at the craft fair. If 6 students entered craft projects, how many did each student sell? How many extra projects did one of the students sell?

7. Misty and 8 of her friends sold a total of 20 boxes of cookies on Saturday. How many boxes did each girl sell? How many extras did one of the girls sell?

8. Troy earned extra money last summer by taking care of 7 different neighbors' homes while they were on vacation. He visited their homes a total of 50 times. How many visits did he make to each house? How many additional visits did he make to one house that had extra flowers to water?

9. Ann decided to sell 46 ears of corn that she grew in her garden. She sold a total of 9 bags. How many ears were in each bag? How many extras did she have for one of the bags?

LET'S SPLIT THESE UP!

1. Mrs. Pink asked her students to divide into groups of 9 to practice speaking their parts for the play. If there were 28 students in her class, how many groups were they able to make? How many students were left over?

   3 R1

2. During recess, 10 girls went out to jump rope. They divided into groups of 3. How many groups did they make, and how many girls were left over?

   3 R1

3. There were 34 students in science class. The teacher asked them to gather into groups of 4 to do an experiment. How many groups did they make, and how many students were left over?

   8 R2

4. In the cafeteria, 44 students were enjoying their lunches. If 8 students were allowed to sit at each table, how many tables were there, and how many students were at the remaining table?

   5 R4

Division of Whole Numbers

5. During art class, 5 students were allowed at each table to paint. If there were 23 students in the class, how many tables were used with 5 students at them? How many students were working at the extra table?

   `4 R3`

6. During recess, the 19 students in Mr. Schmitt's class divided in half to play kickball. How many students were in each group, and how many were left over?

   `9 R1`

7. There was a total of 7 students in Robert's math group. The teacher gave them 45 problems to divide up equally and work out. How many problems did each student do, and how many problems were left over?

   `6 R3`

8. 47 boys and girls in concert choir were asked to divide up into groups of 5 to work on scenery. How many groups of 5 were there, and how many students were in the extra group?

   `9 R2`

9. There are 39 students in the astronomy club that meets on Saturday nights. If there are 6 telescopes, what number of students share each telescope? How many students are left over to join another group?

   `6 R3`

Word Problems IF0193

THERE'S ALWAYS SOMETHING GOING ON AT SCHOOL!

1. There are 89 students that are new this year at Doug's school. If they are placed into 8 classrooms, how many will go in each room? How many will be left over to place?

   12 R3

2. Mr. Fugelhorn had 84 sheets of music to pass out. Each musician received 2 sheets. How many students did he have in his band?

   42

3. Tammy's school just bought 88 new adventure books to read! If each classroom received 7 books, how many classrooms got new books to read? How many were left over to pass out?

   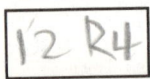
   12 R4

4. There was a total of 39 characters in the after-school play group. If each student played 3 different characters, how many actors were there in the play altogether?

   13

Division of Whole Numbers

5. In Michelle's school, 79 new computers were added to the classrooms. If 6 were added to each room, how many classrooms received them? How many were remaining for the office to use?
   13 R1

6. The P.T.A. bought 65 new playground balls for the school. If each room received 3, how many classrooms received playground balls? How many were left over?
   21 R2

7. The teachers counted a total of 56 poetry entries in the winter poetry contest. If each student who entered submitted 4 poems, how many students entered the contest?
   14

8. David brought 37 treats for his birthday. Each student in the class received 2 treats. How many students received crunchy munchies to enjoy? How many were left over for the teacher?
   18 R1

9. A total of 60 model rockets was made by the astronaut club at Jeff's school. If each member made 5 rockets, how many kids are in the club?
   12

Word Problems IF0193

OUTDOORS CAN BE FUN TOO!

1. 228 boys and girls showed up to become young aeronauts! If 3 children could ride in each hot air balloon at one time, how many balloons were needed to serve everyone?

   76

2. At the park, 144 excited students rode the roller coaster. The roller coaster only carried 6 students at a time. How many times did it have to go around the track to carry all 144 students?

   24

3. A total of 112 students got into groups of 5 to go horseback riding through the forest. How many groups were there, and how many students were left over to make a smaller group?

   22 R 2

4. 571 scouts met at school to start their exciting hiking trip up Moon Peak! Nine buses were used to transport them there. What equal number of scouts rode each bus, and how many were left over to scoot in where there was room?

   63 R 4

Division of Whole Numbers

5. A total of 245 students from Sheree's school went on the overnight to camp. If there were 7 classrooms that went, what was the equal number of students from each classroom?

   35

6. 188 students from Jeremy's school jumped into the tour train at the zoo! Since 4 students rode in each car, how many cars were needed to seat all of the students?

   47

7. All 179 boys and girls on the field trip wanted to ride the miniature cars. Two students were allowed in each car at one time. How many cars were needed in all to give everyone a ride, and how many students were left over?

   89 R1

8. There was a total of 350 students that got to ride on the fire truck. If the fire truck made 8 trips, how many students rode on each trip? How many were left over for the final ride?

   43 R6

9. A total of 401 students from the fourth, fifth and sixth grades went to the park to ride on the large paddle boats. Six students rode on each boat. How many boats were used, and how many students were left over to ride on the extra boat?

   66 R5

Word Problems IF0193

SPECIAL EVENTS FOR KIDS!

1. Since there were 706 students outside ready to play tug of war, they needed to be divided into 2 groups. How many students were on each side of the rope?

   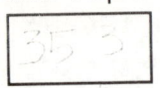

2. The coach said that 859 balloons needed to be filled with water for Field Day. He asked that each student fill 6 balloons. How many students helped fill them? How many were left over to fill?

   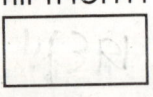

3. There were 751 boys and girls that wanted to be part of the relay races at Peter's school. If each team had 4 students on it, how many teams were they able to make? How many were left over?

4. There were 939 ribbons to be given away at the city swim meet. If each swimmer that participated earned 7 ribbons, how many swimmers were at the meet? How many ribbons were left over?

Division of Whole Numbers

5. A total of 950 miles was run at the citywide fun run. If each boy and girl ran 2 miles, how many children were at the fun run?

6. There was a total of 923 colorful prizes to be handed out to all the boys and girls that came to the holiday carnival. If each child was given 8 prizes, how many boys and girls came to the carnival? How many prizes were left over to be given away?

7. Jennifer's school wanted to make 970 awards for all the hard-working students there. If the students each received 5 awards for all their effort, how many students received awards?

8. What delicious creations came forth at the cookie-making contest! 843 cookies were entered in this exciting event. If the children each entered 3 of their best cookies, how many children participated in this adventurous competition?

9. The fourth grade made a total of 536 drawings for the art show. If each student drew 4 of them, how many submitted drawings?

LET'S HAVE FUN AT SCHOOL!

✗ 1. After school, the math class played a game using 64 multiplication cards! Each student was given 6 cards. How many students played this game? How many cards were left over?

2. There were 96 sheets of paper to draw cartoons on. Each student received 9 sheets. How many students were drawing cartoons? How many sheets were left over to use next time?

10 R6

3. 620 balls were shared by 3 schools. How many did each school receive? How many were left over?

✗ 4. One of the fourth grade teachers found 692 Popsicle sticks to build bridges with. All 3 classrooms wanted to build one, so they divided up the sticks. How many sticks did each room receive, and how many were left over?

Division of Whole Numbers

5. The children threw the Frisbee™ 102 times. If each child threw it 5 times, how many children got to spin it through the air? How many extra throws did one student get?

   `20 R2`

6. Bill's teacher popped a total of 841 pieces of popcorn. Two classes were going to share this popcorn. How many pieces of popcorn did each class receive? How many pieces were left over?

   `42 R1`

7. Pepper's school had 843 sheets of colorful tissue paper to share with 8 classes. How many sheets of paper did each classroom receive? How many were left over?

   `105 R3`

8. The teacher had a total of 82 flash cards to use while the students played a version of Around the World. Each child had a chance to answer 4 cards. How many students played this game? How many flash cards were left to use next time?

   `20 R2`

9. 203 math crossword puzzles were done by the 2 fourth grade classrooms. Each student finished 4 puzzles. How many students had fun doing these puzzles, and how many were left over?

   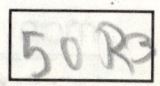
   `50 R3`

Word Problems IF0193

LARGE NUMBERS DIVIDE UP JUST AS EASILY!

1. Three schools brought in a total of 4,272 different things for the rummage sale. How many items did each school bring in?

   ☐

2. 5,632 letters were sent to the President from 2 schools near Bobby's house. They wanted to say "Hi!" and let him know what a great job he is doing. How many letters did each school send?

   ☐

3. The cafeteria at Eva's school has served 2,716 hamburgers. The five different times they were on the menu, the kids loved them. How many hamburgers were served each day they were on the menu? How many extras were served one day?

   ☐

4. Student newsletters have been sent home from Lori's school 6 different times totaling 4,284. There are many exciting things going on there. How many newsletters were sent each time?

   ☐

Division of Whole Numbers

5. 8,606 flyers were sent out advertising the new space museum near Samuel's school. If the same amount was sent out 4 different times, how many flyers were sent out each time? How many extras were sent out?

6. Seven elementary schools came out for the citywide Kite Day! They brought a total of 2,501 kites that zoomed and glided blissfully through the air. How many kites did each school bring? How many extras did one school bring?

7. A total of 8,204 students from all over the city marched and played instruments joyfully in the celebration parade. Five school districts were represented. How many band members came from each district? How many extras came?

8. A total of 2,168 students came out on 4 different days to see the space shuttle exhibit. How many students came each day?

9. There were 9,308 singers that came from the towns of Frog Hop and Elbow Creek to join in on the Fourth of July celebration. How many singers came from each town?

FUN FOODS ARE JUST PLAIN "FUN!"

1. For his going away party, Rafael brought in 57 tamales for the 25 students in his class. How many tamales did each child receive? How many extras were left over to give to his favorite teachers?

   2 R 7

2. The P.T.A. gave the 2 fourth grade classes a total of 73 pretzels for reading the most books. How many students were in each class, and how many extras were in one class?

   36 R 1

3. The P.E. coach shared a total of 93 yogurt bars with the different field hockey teams at school. Each team had 15 players. How many teams were there? How many yogurt bars were left over?

   6 R 3

4. 77 beef jerky sticks were brought as a treat for all the helpers that painted the music room. There were 23 children from each room that came to help. How many classrooms painted the music room? How many sticks were left over?

   3 R 8

Division of Whole Numbers

5. 75 ears of popcorn were brought to the meeting for the scouts to plant. If each den had a total of 18 scouts, how many dens were there to receive the special ears of popcorn? How many ears were left over?

   4 R3

6. Jim ordered 93 cups to use to serve ice cream to the fourth graders. If there were 30 children in each class, how many classrooms would be enjoying ice cream? How many extra cups would they have?

   3 R3

7. The cafeteria at camp served 97 apples to the children after dinner as a snack. If each cabin had 13 children in it, how many cabins were served apples after dinner? How many were left over?

   7 R6

8. 90 cups of warm tea were put out for the choirs that performed. If each choir had 42 members, how many choirs enjoyed warm tea before performing? How many extra cups were there?

   2 R6

9. The fourth grade teachers brought in a total of 67 potatoes to make potato prints. If there was a total of 21 students in each classroom, how many classrooms got to make potato prints? How many extra potatoes did they have?

   3 R4

DIVISION TAKES PLACE OUTSIDE OF CLASS TOO!

1. Earl brought 320 marbles to school to share. He gave each of his friends 62 marbles. How many friends did he share marbles with? How many extras did he have?

2. Calvin's school passed out 251 balloons on Math Celebration Day! Each classroom received 31 balloons. How many classes got balloons? How many were left over?

3. The cafeteria offered cactus candy to those that might want to try it! The tray had 314 pieces on it. 47 children from each grade level tried the candy. How many grade levels tasted it? How many pieces were left over?

4. 204 math champion certificates were ordered for those students that knew all their multiplication facts to the twelve's. How many grade levels each received 53 certificates? How many were left to give out later?

Division of Whole Numbers

5. The office brought out 516 pencils for the big crossword puzzle event at John's school. If each class got 21 pencils, how many classes were there? How many pencils were left over?

6. There were 750 ribbons purchased for the swimmers from around the city that swam in the summer swimming program. If 92 students from each school enjoyed the summer swimming program, how many schools entered? How many ribbons were left over?

7. Archie's dad brought in 373 football cards of himself and other members of his team in the National Football League. If each child was given 13 autographed cards, how many children received these unique gifts? How many cards were left over?

8. The grocery store near school delivered 554 paper bags for the students to color and decorate! If each student decorated 15 paper bags, how many students helped make this store a more colorful place? How many extra bags were left over for those that wanted to draw more?

WHAT IS YOUR FAVORITE?

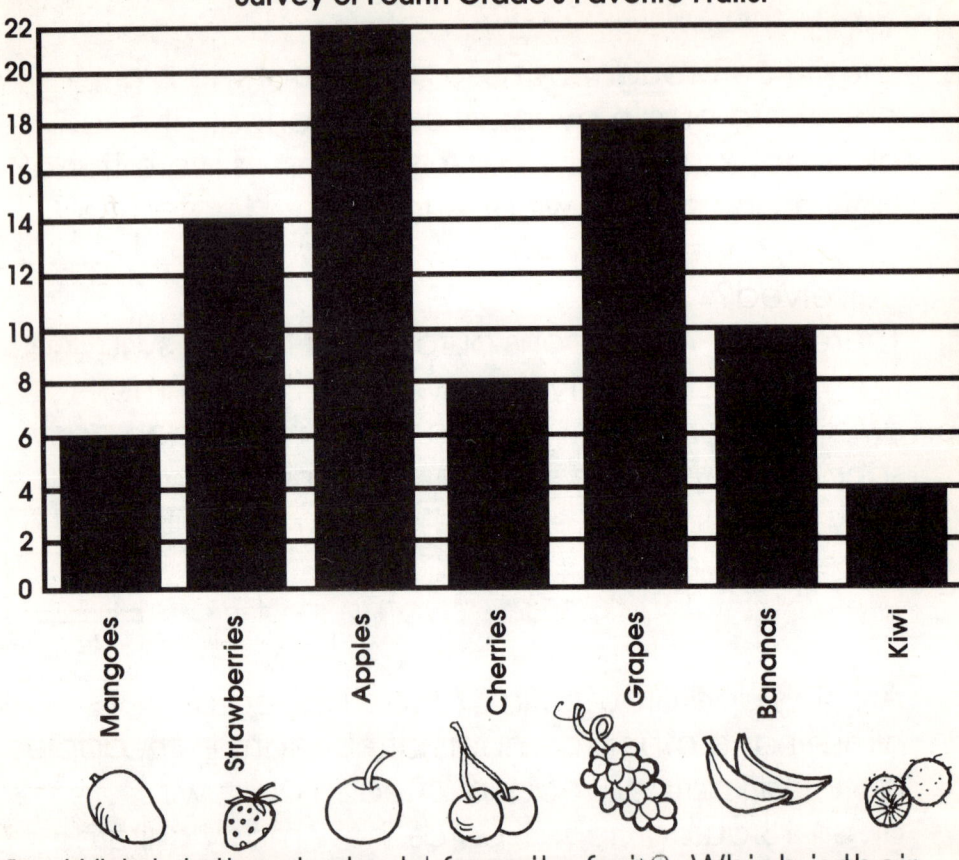

1. Which is the students' favorite fruit? Which is their least favorite?

2. How many more students voted for apples than strawberries?

3. If 3 classrooms voted, and each room cast the same amount of votes for grapes, how many votes did each room cast?

Using a Bar Graph

4. What is the total number of votes that apples, strawberries and grapes received?

5. If 9 times the number of students had voted for grapes, how many votes would grapes have received?

6. Which is greater, the sum of apple and strawberry votes, or the sum of grape and strawberry votes?

7. How many fourth graders voted in all?

8. How many more times did students vote for apples than they did for mangoes?

9. What is the difference in range between the fruit that received the greatest amount of votes and the one that received the least amount of votes?

FIELD TRIPS ARE SUCH A BLAST!

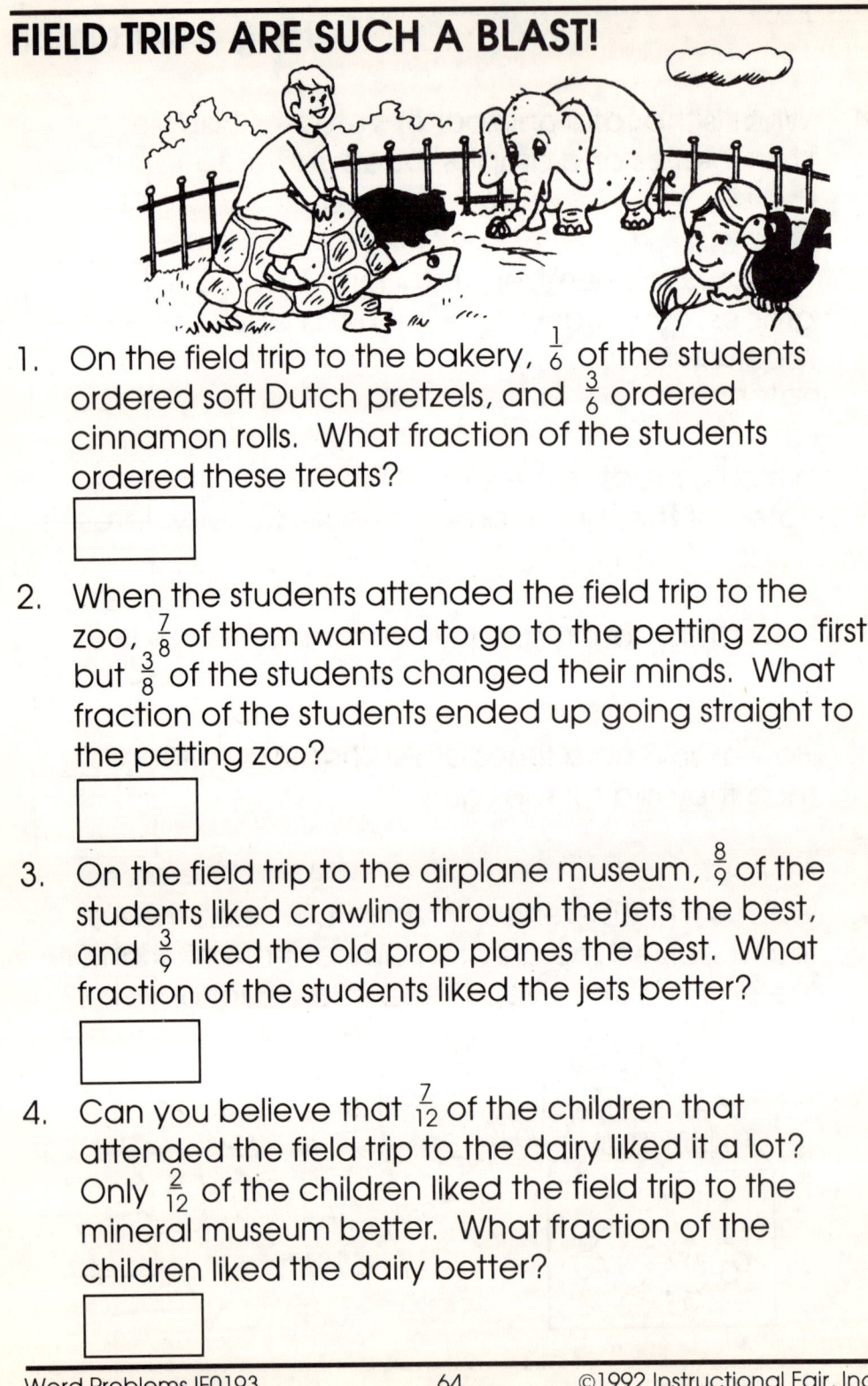

1. On the field trip to the bakery, $\frac{1}{6}$ of the students ordered soft Dutch pretzels, and $\frac{3}{6}$ ordered cinnamon rolls. What fraction of the students ordered these treats?

2. When the students attended the field trip to the zoo, $\frac{7}{8}$ of them wanted to go to the petting zoo first, but $\frac{3}{8}$ of the students changed their minds. What fraction of the students ended up going straight to the petting zoo?

3. On the field trip to the airplane museum, $\frac{8}{9}$ of the students liked crawling through the jets the best, and $\frac{3}{9}$ liked the old prop planes the best. What fraction of the students liked the jets better?

4. Can you believe that $\frac{7}{12}$ of the children that attended the field trip to the dairy liked it a lot? Only $\frac{2}{12}$ of the children liked the field trip to the mineral museum better. What fraction of the children liked the dairy better?

Addition and Subtraction of Fractions

5. On the class picnic, $\frac{2}{10}$ of the students brought bread to feed the ducks, and $\frac{4}{10}$ wanted to throw Frisbees™. What fraction of the boys and girls wanted to feed the ducks or throw Frisbees™?

6. The students learned on their trip to the fish hatchery that $\frac{3}{6}$ of the fish raised there are trout and $\frac{2}{6}$ of them are bass. What fraction of these two fish are raised at the hatchery?

7. Mrs. Blink's class found out that $\frac{6}{11}$ of all the musicians that go to the recording studio play guitar and piano. Woodwind instruments are played by $\frac{3}{11}$ that go there. What fraction of these musicians plays these types of instruments?

8. While Mrs. Valentine's class was visiting the art museum, $\frac{7}{10}$ of the exhibits were paintings. Only $\frac{1}{10}$ of them were sculptures. What greater fraction of the exhibits were paintings?

9. On the swimming trip, $\frac{2}{5}$ of the students liked the high dive, and $\frac{1}{5}$ of the students preferred the low dive. What greater fraction of the students liked the high dive?

AND THE FRACTION IS . . .

1. To make fossils, Suzanne measured out $3\frac{1}{4}$ cups of plaster of Paris. Then she measured out $8\frac{2}{4}$ cups of water. How many cups of plaster and water did she measure out?

2. Rose Anne measured out $11\frac{4}{5}$ cups of flour to make salt dough for her puppet project. Then she decided it was too much and took out $3\frac{2}{5}$ cups of the flour. How much flour did she end up using?

3. Peter's father wanted to buy $13\frac{4}{8}$ gallons of gas for his truck. After he realized how much money he had, he ended up buying $8\frac{2}{8}$ gallons less. How many gallons of gas did he end up buying?

4. Jim's cat weighed a total of $18\frac{3}{10}$ pounds. His lizard weighed $5\frac{1}{10}$ pounds. How much more did his cat weigh?

Addition and Subtraction of Mixed Numerals

5. Tammy weighed out $6\frac{4}{12}$ ounces of gourmet fish for her cat. Then she measured out $4\frac{3}{12}$ ounces of liver-flavored dry cat food. How many ounces of food in all did her cat have for dinner?

6. Eileen's dog weighed a total of $3\frac{1}{6}$ kilograms. Anthony's dog weighed a total of $9\frac{3}{6}$ kilograms. How much did their dogs weigh altogether?

7. The people at Donny's house just love milk. They drink about $5\frac{2}{10}$ gallons each week. Heather and her family love milk too, but they only drink about $3\frac{1}{10}$ gallons each week. How much more milk does Donny's family drink?

8. Francis can't believe that he uses about $35\frac{7}{12}$ gallons of water to take a shower. Nor can he believe that he uses about $2\frac{4}{12}$ gallons of water to brush his teeth. How much water does he use altogether for these two things?

9. Bobby found out that his books weigh $4\frac{3}{8}$ kilograms. Marie couldn't believe that her books weigh $3\frac{4}{8}$ kilograms. How much weight in all do they carry to school each morning?

HAVE FUN WITH THESE!

1. All 9 boys at the sleepover were 12 years old. How many years does that add up to altogether?

2. The city newspaper printed 68,328 copies of the morning edition and 43,895 copies of the evening edition. How many copies were printed in all?

3. At skate night, $\frac{8}{12}$ of the students liked having the special "backward skate" during the last skate of the night. But $\frac{3}{12}$ of the students didn't want to have it at all. What greater fraction of the students wanted to have a "backward skate" session?

4. Seven students each reached the goal of finishing 2,641 math problems at school this year. How many problems did this total in all?

Choosing the Operation

5. Nine students at Tina's school signed up for the special science magazine subscription. If each subscription sold for $14.78, how much did it cost them altogether?

6. During recess, a group of boys found 58 rocks that would work perfectly for their story characters during creative writing. If each boy picked out 8, how many boys were going to use these rocks to write creative stories? How many rocks would be left over?

7. The packages that Billy had to mail to France weighed 63.91 grams, 4.82 grams and 50.27 grams. How many grams did they weigh altogether?

8. There was a total of 8,146 beehives at 3 different sites on Larry's family's farm. What equal number of hives were at each site? How many extras were at one site?

9. A total of 42 home runs was hit by 8 of the boys on the baseball teams during the season. How many home runs did each boy hit? How many extra home runs did one of the boys hit?

HERE'S A CHALLENGE FOR YOU!

1. Eight classrooms had the opportunity to see the reptile exhibit that came to school. There were 29 students in each classroom. How many students in all got to experience the exhibit?

2. 507 students ordered the freshly baked chicken from the school cafeteria for lunch. Only 239 brought their own lunches. How many more students ordered the delicious school lunch?

3. Cheryl's school collected $5\frac{1}{4}$ tons of newspaper for recycling. Jim's school collected $4\frac{2}{4}$ tons. How many tons of newspaper did the schools collect in all?

4. Seven times, Gwen had to order 38.60 kilograms of dog food for the pet store. How many kilograms of dog food did she order altogether?

Choosing the Operation

5. The bookstore donated a total of 213 exciting and adventurous books to the 5 fourth grades at Mark's school. How many books did each classroom receive? How many extras were there?

6. Last month when the new gyro toy came out, Jack's Toy Store sold 86,924 of them. This month, sales are down to 19,283. How many more of the gyro toys did the store sell the first month?

7. 246 bicycle clubs around America each decided to give out 382 "riding safely" awards to those boys and girls that they see doing a great job following safety rules. How many awards will be given out in all?

8. Steven's school ordered 278 math champion awards for the 9 classrooms in the upper grades. How many awards did each teacher receive to hand out to those that earned them? How many extra awards did the school have?

9. Kimberly saved $83.47 to buy a new easel to paint on! The one she picked out cost $59.92. How much money did she have left?

HELP-AT-HOME ACTIVITIES

Below are some activities to do with your child at home.

1. Take a picture of your child. Write height and weight on back. Repeat once a month. Write problems to compare the heights and weights.
2. Write 25¢ five different ways.
3. Do 4 math problems using something in your kitchen. Example: 11 beans minus 5 beans equals?
4. Read a newspaper article that deals with numbers. Make up problems with the numbers.
5. Play popcorn math. Example: Have 20 🍿, you ate 11 🍿. How many are left over?
6. Measure a room together.
7. Write the even numbers from 100 backward to 0.
8. Write a math word problem whose answer is equal to today's date.
9. Figure out how many minutes he/she will be awake today.
10. Give your child a ruler to measure his/her foot, hand, arm, etc.
11. Figure out how many days there are until his/her birthday.
12. Use candy to make math problems.
13. Draw 2 clocks representing when your child gets up in the morning and goes to bed at night.
14. Use holiday themes to make up word problems. Example: 12 gingerbread men ate 9 candy canes each. How many candy canes was this altogether?
15. Look at a recipe. Have him/her double and triple the recipe.